CLAY
CHARACTERS
for KIDS

Maureen Carlson

NORTH LIGHT BOOKS
CINCINNATI, OHIO
www.artistsnetwork.com

About the Author

Maureen Carlson remembers that her mother never let her or her brother and sister say, "I'm bored!" According to her, being bored meant that you weren't being creative about the way you used your time. "Nothing to do? How could that be?" There were always art supplies around, and of course there were books and pets and all of the outdoors. And if that failed, there were always dishes to wash! Or gardens to weed!

Maureen is the author of *How to Make Clay Characters* and *Family and Friends in Polymer Clay*, both from North Light Books. She and her husband, Dan, own a polymer clay mail-order company called Wee Folk Creations. In 2002, Maureen Carlson's Center for Creative Arts opened in Jordan, Minnesota. Maureen has written for numerous craft magazines and has produced a series of instructional videotapes about polymer clay. Her push molds and figurines are found in craft and gift stores nationwide.

Maureen Carlson as a child, on the right, with her longtime friend, Karen Summer Short. (Picture taken in the mid 1950s by AnaBel Peck.)

Clay Characters for Kids. © 2003 by Maureen Carlson. Manufactured in China. All rights reserved. No part of this book may be reproduced in any form or by any electronic or mechanical means including information storage and retrieval systems without permission in writing from the publisher, except by a reviewer, who may quote brief passages in a review. Published by North Light Books, an imprint of F+W Publications, Inc., 4700 East Galbraith Road, Cincinnati, Ohio 45236. (800) 289-0963. First edition.

Other fine North Light Books are available from your local bookstore or art supply store or direct from the publisher.

17 16 15 14 13   15 14 13 12 11

Library of Congress Cataloging-in-Publication Data
Carlson, Maureen
    Clay characters for kids / Maureen Carlson.
      p.cm.
    Summary: Provides an introduction to polymer clay and instructions for creating basic shapes and using them to make characters that appear in the accompanying story, "The Magic of Storyclay."
    ISBN-13: 978-1-58180-286-3 (alk. paper)
    ISBN-10: 1-58180-286-2 (alk. paper)
    1. Polymer clay craft—Juvenile literature. [1. Clay modeling. 2. Handicraft.] I. Title.
TT297 .C268 2002
731.4'2—dc21   2002067776

Editors: Maggie Moschell and Christine Doyle
Designer: Stephanie Strang
Production artist: Donna Cozatchy
Production coordinator: Kristen Heller
Photographers: Maureen Carlson (all interior photos), additional photography by AnaBel Peck and Christine Polomsky
Cover photography by Al Parrish
Cover photo styling by Jan Nickum

Storyclay ® Telling is a registered trademark of Maureen Carlson.

F+W PUBLICATIONS, INC.

metric conversion chart

TO CONVERT	TO	MULTIPLY BY
Inches	Centimeters	2.54
Centimeters	Inches	0.4
Feet	Centimeters	30.5
Centimeters	Feet	0.03
Yards	Meters	0.9
Meters	Yards	1.1
Sq. Inches	Sq. Centimeters	6.45
Sq. Centimeters	Sq. Inches	0.16
Sq. Feet	Sq. Meters	0.09
Sq. Meters	Sq. Feet	10.8
Sq. Yards	Sq. Meters	0.8
Sq. Meters	Sq. Yards	1.2
Pounds	Kilograms	0.45
Kilograms	Pounds	2.2
Ounces	Grams	28.4
Grams	Ounces	0.04

Dedication

I grew up on a farm near Elsie, Michigan, where my best friend, Karen, and I attended a one-room country school named Page School. For all nine of my years in that school, Karen was the only other girl in my class. We both loved recess, reading and art. We raced through our work in order to get back to the books we were reading or to our creative projects.

Page School became a gallery for the students. The school was the center of community activities and was a regular meeting place for community potlucks and ice cream socials and box suppers—all of which required the room to be decorated. I remember feeling proud and excited when everyone's family came to see what we had been doing in our school.

The years went on, and both Karen and I moved away from Elsie—Karen to become a nurse and I to become a teacher. But I am still that little girl who loves stories and colors and paper and scissors and the wonderful joy of creating something new.

Karen, together we hold the memories of our child selves.
We grew up together and helped each other become who we are.
Without your intelligence, abilities, gentleness and friendship, I might have settled for being less. You challenged me, encouraged me and believed in me. Being 5 and 6 and on up to 14 with a constant best friend is just about as good as it gets.
This book is for you.

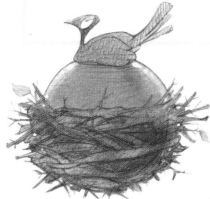

A Big Thank-You to: Teachers and youth leaders everywhere—in and out of schools—who make an effort to really see and listen to the thoughts and ideas of kids. I believe that all people—young and old and in between—need to feel safe and accepted in order to be free to create with joy and abandon.

Maggie Moschell, who deserves a big, shiny medal that reads "The Encourager." She made this book happen with her patience, intuitive wisdom and humor. I will make that T-shirt that says, "So many ideas, so little time."

Lu Christoph, who helped with the clay models and who keeps my Center for Creative Arts in Jordan, Minnesota, together so that I can keep creating.

Laura Normile, age 10, who patiently and cheerfully served as my hand model.

My family, without whom none of my work would have heart.

table of

CONTENTS

A Note to
Grown-Ups

Adult Supervision Needed

Most children find polymer clay extremely easy to use. However, an adult must closely supervise baking the clay. Your supervision is also needed for the dragon project on page 70 which benefits from the use of a sharp blade to slice the dragon's scales.

Getting Started

* Read pages 8 and 9 with your child to be sure that he or she understands the safety precautions and helpful tips for using polymer clay.

* Wash hands thoroughly after handling polymer clay. Some clays will stain your hands. It's a good idea to keep a box of disposable alcohol-free wipes handy to clean hands between colors. Waterless hand cleaners also work.

* Protect painted and varnished surfaces, plus carpeted areas, from unbaked clay.

* One of the most exciting things to do with polymer clay is mixing colors. You'll have less clay waste and better results if you help your child understand the principles of color mixing on pages 12 and 13. But don't throw out those inevitable muddy gray blobs! They make great rocks and animals.

* Page 10 gives tips on warming, softening and kneading ("conditioning") the clay. It usually becomes soft and malleable quite quickly, but some clays are stiffer than others. Your child may need your help with conditioning because your hands may be warmer and stronger.

* Be sure that your child has a set of tools that are just for polymer clay. Once a tool, such as a rolling pin, is used for clay, it should not be used again for food.

* Polymer clay doesn't dry out, but it's a good idea to store the colors in separate plastic bags to keep them clean. Store clay at room temperature and away from high-heat sources, such as heating ducts and direct sunlight.

Baking Polymer Clay

* Bake clay projects on a ceramic tile, cookie sheet or aluminum pan. Insulated or doubled pans help protect the bottoms from scorching, especially if the oven has hot spots. Lining the pan with white paper, baking parchment, aluminum foil or an index card helps to keep your pans clean.

* An adult should always supervise baking clay. Follow the directions on the clay package. Use a regular oven, convection oven or toaster oven, but not a microwave. Most clays are baked at 265° to 275° F (129° to 135°C), depending on the brand. A separate oven thermometer is recommended to ensure that the oven is at the proper temperature.

* Underbaked clay is weak and may break. Overbaked clay may scorch. If the clay scorches, open a window to remove the fumes.

* Baked clay can have unbaked clay added to it and then be baked again. This is useful for adding details. However, care must be used because some clays scorch more easily than others. If the clay starts to turn brown, remove it from the oven.

* When the baking is finished, turn off the oven, open the door and let the project cool in the oven. Otherwise, be very careful when you remove it from the oven. Hot clay is fragile.

* Polymer clay hardens to a matte finish when baked. If your child wants a glossy surface, paint the project with a matte or glossy lacquer made especially for polymer clay. Some clear varnishes will not dry on polymer clay.

imagination
TIME

Here's a poem to get you started on your **adventures** with **polymer clay!**

W hat do you see when you look in this basket?

(It must be a trick or she wouldn't have asked it!)

I see a blue-eyed girl and a freckle-faced elf

Having tea with a princess who looks like herself!

T wo fairies, a goblin, a wizard and a troll

Are using a pumpkin to learn how to bowl.

A dd three grinning cats and four barking dogs…

Plus a horse, a cow and three fat frogs.

I close my eyes
and count to ten

And up pops a pig
and three fat hens.

Swimming through
all this noisy mess

Are six bright fish
and a turtle playing chess.

Watching over
the whole grand scene

Is a pair of dragons,
a king and a queen.

follow the rules for
POLYMER CLAY

You, too, can make "magic"
from plain lumps of clay!
It's true, you can do it. Now what do you say?

All that is needed for you to begin
Is some clay and some tools and the will to dig in.

But wait, before starting, it's important to say:
Follow the rules each time you use clay!

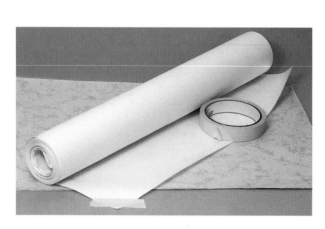

Clean your hands before you begin.

Don't eat while working with clay.

Keep your clay tools *separate* from those used for food. Once your tools have been used with clay, they shouldn't be used for food.

Protect your work surface with freezer paper or a plastic mat.

Use aluminum foil for the insides of clay pieces that are bigger than a small plum. The pieces will bake more evenly and you will save on clay. Crumple up the foil, then cover it with clay.

Toothpicks or wire placed in the center of thin pieces will give them extra strength. This is also a good way to hold parts together.

Prop your pieces up with index cards so they won't tip over while baking.

Have an adult help *bake your clay* projects on a baking sheet, clay tile or foil pan. Baking on an index card, aluminum foil, parchment paper or a piece of cardstock will keep your pan clean.

Use a timer so that you don't overbake your clay. If you have time, cool the polymer clay in the oven with the door open. Why? So you won't be tempted to pick up your creation too soon! Also, hot polymer clay breaks very easily.

safety tip...

Keep paper pieces away from the heating coils or elements in the oven. Paper does not burn at 265° to 275° F (129° to 135° C), but heating elements themselves may get hotter than that.

Store polymer clay in plastic bags, one bag for each color.

working with
POLYMER CLAY

Warming Up
Your Clay

When you open a new pack-
age of clay it may feel hard
or crumbly because it is
cold. Warming and mixing
polymer clay is called
"conditioning"
the clay. Each brand
of clay will have a slightly
different feel, but all should
get soft if properly condi-
tioned. Warm the clay in
your hands for a few min-
utes, or put it in a plastic

bag and sit on it. When the
clay is warm, squeeze it, roll
it around, and twist it until
it gets soft enough to use.

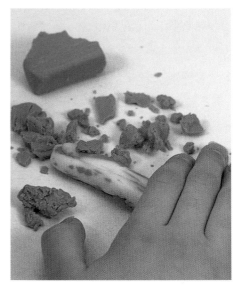

Warm clay that is still crumbly may be old,
or it may have been stored in a hot place. Try
adding some Mix Quick kneading medium, or
add a softer clay to the hard clay. Roll the
soft clay through the hard pieces to pick
them up, then twist and mix, until it is soft.

Tools
You Can Use

Tools are not needed. Well, hardly at all.
It only takes hands to roll logs and make balls.

But things like a roller, a cutter and picks
Are handy additions to your bag of clay tricks!

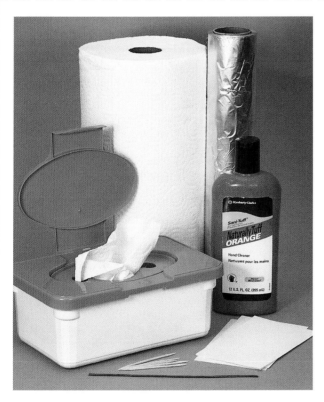

clay roller

brayer

dull knife

knitting needle

wooden tool set

While your hands are all you need to work with clay, some tools will be useful as you make the projects in this book. Some good tools to have are pictured here.

paintbrushes

empty pen shaft

straw

toothpicks

Keep these supplies on hand for baking and clean-up: (clockwise, from left) disposable alcohol-free wipes; paper towels; aluminum foil; waterless hand cleaner; index cards; wire; and toothpicks.

So Many Colors

So many colors and so hard to choose.
For most I take one, but white—always two.

With white as a base I mix colors galore.
Wow! Many more colors than ever before!

Mixing colors is easy. It needn't be tough.
But without a few tips, it is kind of rough.

For colors mixed any old this way and that,
Soon look like the color of Granddad's old hat.

There are three primary colors: red, yellow and blue.
All other colors are made from a mix of these colors. Mixing a primary color with the one next to it creates secondary colors, which are orange, purple and green. Mixing again with the next-door color creates many new colors (blue-green, yellow-orange, and red-violet), and so on, and on, and on!

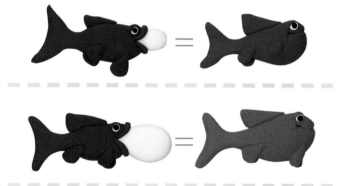

Adding white makes a color lighter.

The more white you add, the lighter the color will be.

hint...
Save your scraps to mix new **colors. Even muddy gray colors are useful for making rocks or animals.**

To make a color muddier or less bright,
add a bit of the color that's on the opposite side of the color wheel.

Mixing Colors

1
To mix colors quickly, put two different colored pieces of clay together and make a rope (see page 20).

2
Then fold and twist the rope.

3
Knead, roll and fold again.

4
Repeat step 3. First you will get stripes, then a solid color. If you like the stripes, stop! If not, keep mixing.

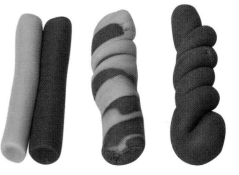

Some colors mixed together will surprise you. Remember, colors that are opposite each other on the color wheel create muddy colors when mixed.

Making a Striped Rope

1
To create bold stripes, make two ropes. Lay them side by side.

2
Twist loosely.

3
Then continue twisting by holding one hand steady and pulling one toward you.

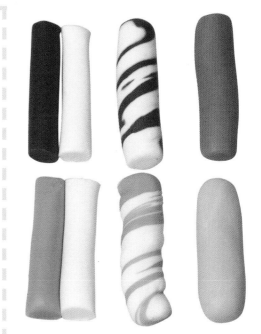

When making stripes or new colors, practice with white as your second color. If you mess it up, you will still have your basic clay color.

making
SHAPES

Every clay artist has a bag of clay tricks. It cannot be seen, not like mortar or bricks.
This bag is invisible. It sits in your head Like all of the words from the books you have read.
But when you need shapes to make bears or make hearts,
Just look in your bag and you'll know how to start!

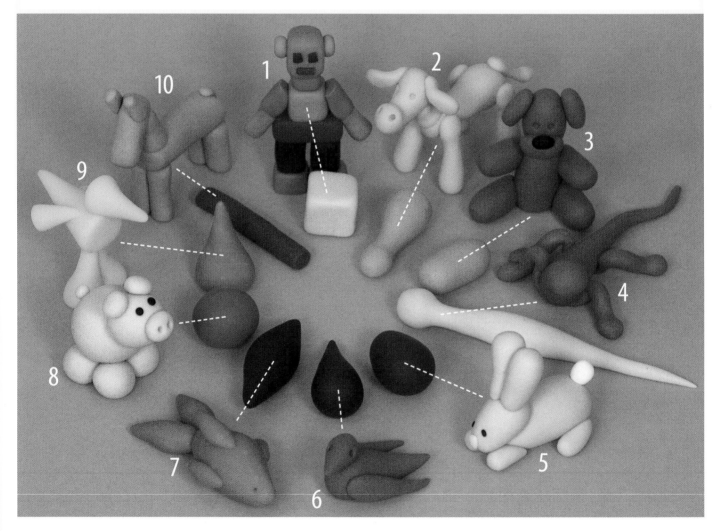

Each of these characters can be made with one of ten basic shapes. If you can make these ten shapes, you can make anything shown in this book.

1 A robot made with cubes.
2 A cowdog made with drumstick shapes.
3 A dog made with ovals.
4 A lizard made with ghost shapes.
5 A bunny made with egg shapes.

6 A bird made with teardrop shapes.
7 A fish made with football shapes.
8 A pig made with balls.
9 A bird made with cones.
10 A horse made with rope shapes.

Balls

1 Every shape in this book begins with a ball. To make a ball, roll the clay around and around in the palms of your hands. Rolling a ball is the easiest way to get the wrinkles out of the clay.

2 Does your ball have wrinkles? If the clay is too cold, warm it up! If the clay is too hard, mix in a softer clay. If you aren't rolling hard enough, use a little more energy!

3 Are you having problems making the balls round? You may be pressing too hard, so lighten up! Let it roll freely around your whole palm.

Practice making balls in all different sizes. Then press them together to make an **all-ball pig!**

h i n t ...
Follow the directions for making each character. *Then ask an adult* to bake them following the directions on the package of clay. *Other tips for baking are on page 5.*

Eggs

1

Hold a ball on the table or in one hand.
Hold your other hand at an angle.

2

Roll your hand against one side of the ball to create a pointed end.

Ovals

1

To make an oval, begin with a ball, then roll it back and forth instead of around and around.

2

The ends of the oval are round like the ball, but the oval is longer.

Make this dog with ten ovals of different sizes.

3

Pat the pointed end to make it rounded like the small end of an egg.

Some of the egg bunny's eggs are long, some are short, but all have **rounded ends.**

Teardrops

1

To make a teardrop, begin with a ball, then roll it into an egg.

2

Keep rolling the small end with your hand.

3

Roll the end until it comes to a point.

This bird is made of four teardrops.

Cones

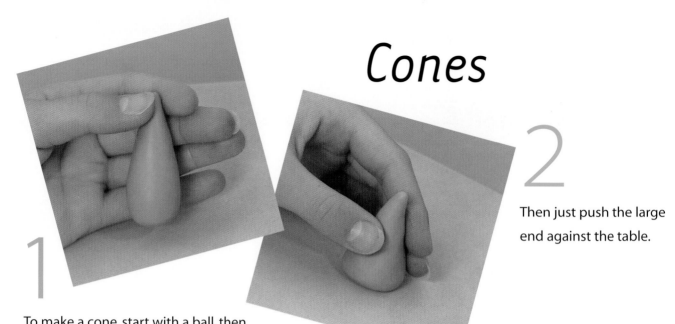

1 To make a cone, start with a ball, then make an egg and a teardrop.

2 Then just push the large end against the table.

Footballs

1 To make a football, begin with a ball, then roll that into an egg and a teardrop.

2 Then make the other end of the teardrop pointed, too. Use your fingers to make the clay pointy.

3 The football is round in the middle and pointed at both ends.

A football shape *seems perfect for this* fish.

3

The cone will have one pointy end and one flat end.

*Here's a **six-cone bird**.*

*What other animals can you make with **cones?***

Drumsticks

1

Begin with a ball, then make an egg. Roll your finger against the egg shape to make a dent.

2

Roll your finger all around the egg.

3

Keep rolling your finger against the egg until it looks like a chicken drumstick.

*This **cowdog** is made of **ten drumstick** shapes.*

hint...
Prop this cowdog over a rolled index card while he's baking. Keep the feet flat on the baking pan so he will stand up after he's baked and cooled.

Ropes

2

1
Even a rope starts out as a ball. Roll the ball into an oval, then roll the oval back and forth to make it longer.

Use two hands to stretch the rope as it gets longer. If your rope is lumpy, don't press so hard, and stretch the rope as you roll it.

Cubes

1
To make a cube, press a ball between four fingers.

2
Turn the ball and press the opposite sides.

3
Flatten the ball still more with your hand. Pressing it gently on the table helps to make the sides flat.

4
Be sure to rotate and do all six sides.

*I couldn't think of an animal made of **cubes**, so I made **a robot**.*

3

Keep rolling until your rope is as long or as thick as you'd like it to be.

*You can make **a horse** out of **ropes**.*
*You could call that **"roping"** the horse!*

Ghosts

1

To make a ghost, begin with a ball, then make an egg. Then turn the egg into a drumstick.

2

Roll your hand against the big end to create a point.

3

Keep rolling and stretching until the point turns into a tail.

4

Twist the tail a bit and add a face (see page 40) and you have a ghost.

***Add** some drumstick legs to **make a lizard**.*

changing the
SHAPES

Other skills for your bag of clay tricks Are ways to use tools like rollers and picks.
So learn how to flatten, to curl and to cut. And you'll never, no never, get stuck in a rut.

Making a
Flattened
Shape

1 Press a shape between your palms or against an index card lying on a table. The card will keep the clay from sticking to the table.

2 Flatten the clay still more by rocking your hand back and forth over the clay.

3 Stretch the clay to make it really thin. Stretch slowly or it will rip!

Another Way

You can also flatten clay with a brayer, rolling pin or pasta machine.

Rolled Flower and Mr. Inchworm
Use what you've learned about flattening shapes to make this project.

1.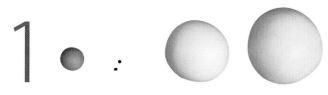

Roll balls for each of the parts of the project. The clay balls on the left are for Mr. Inchworm, and the two on the right are for the flower.

Handy tools:
- toothpick
- scissors
- ceramic mug

2. Roll the stem ball into a teardrop, then a cone. Push a toothpick into the center and use scissors to cut off the extra. Follow the directions on page 5 for baking the stem. Let it cool.

3. Roll the flower ball into a rope or oval, then flatten it. Loosely wrap the flat shape around the baked stem.

4. Use your finger to curl over the flower's edges.

continued on the next page ➡

5 Follow the steps shown here to make Mr. Inchworm. Press him into place on top of the flower.

6 Prop the flower with a ceramic coffee mug while baking. The paper keeps the clay from becoming shiny where it touches the mug. An adult should help you bake it by following the directions on page 5.

Be Creative!

You can change the size of your flowers just by rolling bigger or smaller balls of clay.

Gathered flower

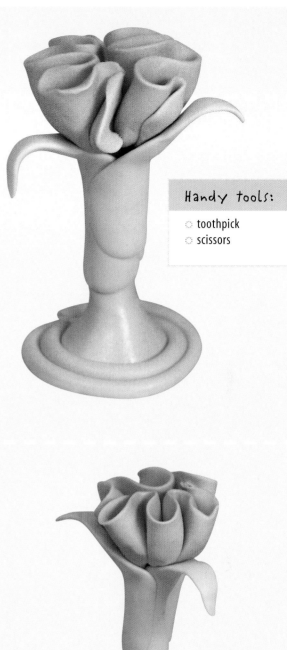

Handy tools:
- toothpick
- scissors

1 Begin by making and baking a stem like you did on page 23. For the petals, roll a ball into a rope. Then flatten the rope and loosely fold it. Make two of these for each flower.

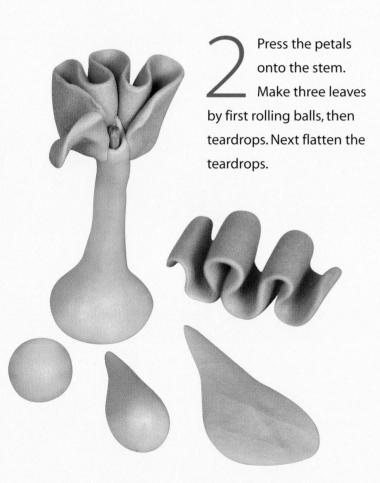

2 Press the petals onto the stem. Make three leaves by first rolling balls, then teardrops. Next flatten the teardrops.

3 Press the rounded end of the leaves to the stem. To balance your stem, wind a clay rope around the base. Bake it by following the directions on page 5.

25

Flat Flower and Dragonfly

Here's another project for you to make using flattened shapes.

1 Make five balls of the same size for the flower petals. Make three smaller balls for the flower's center. Make six balls as shown for Dragonfly. You'll also need colored wire for Dragonfly—I've used green wire.

Handy tools:
- toothpick
- colored wire
- paper clips
- index cards

2 Make a ball for the stem, then roll it into a cone. Push a toothpick into the stem, leaving the end sticking out. Roll the petal balls into teardrops, then flatten them.

3 Flatten the teardrops for Dragonfly's wings, and make the body as shown. Push one end of the wire into Dragonfly's body. Curl the other end into a loop. Press the parts together. Bake Dragonfly and the flower stem according to the directions on page 5, and let them cool.

4 Fold an index card so that it is as tall as the stem. Roll it into a tube and clip it with a paper clip. Place the stem in the center of the tube. Press the small end of each petal onto the toothpick and use the edge of the tube to hold up the petals.

6 Press the stacked center onto the flower. Keep the index card tube in place and bake it following the directions on page 5.

5 Press the looped end of Dragonfly's wire into the center of the flower. The wings will lie flat on the baking surface.

7 When the clay is cool, curl the wire by wrapping it around a pencil or paintbrush handle.

hint... ***If your flower tips over,*** *bend the wire in a different direction or add a rope of clay around the base and bake it again. Remember to prop it on the baking sheet.*

Making a
Quick Turn

1 To make a single quick turn, start with a rope and make a soft bend. Be careful not to flatten the rope. Notice that your fingers should be on the top and sides of the clay rope, not on the bottom.

2 Make a soft point by pressing the clay toward the quick turn.

3 Pat the corner smooth. Practice doing a quick turn, then do several in a row.

This sidewinder's body is a good example of the quick turn. It has fifteen turns!

Sidewinder

Now that you know about quick turns, try making this sidewinder.

1 Begin your sidewinder with a ball. Roll it into an egg, then a drumstick. Roll the large end of the drumstick until it is long and skinny.

Handy tools:
- dull knife or toothpick
- index card
- paper clips

2 Make as many quick turns as you can on the tail.

3 Draw a mouth using the knife (see page 41). Press on clay balls for eyes. Bend the head up, and prop it on the baking sheet with the rolled index card. Bake following the directions on page 5.

Lu the Garden Elf

Use quick turns to make Lu's knees and elbows. To make the flat flower and Dragonfly, follow the instructions on page 26.

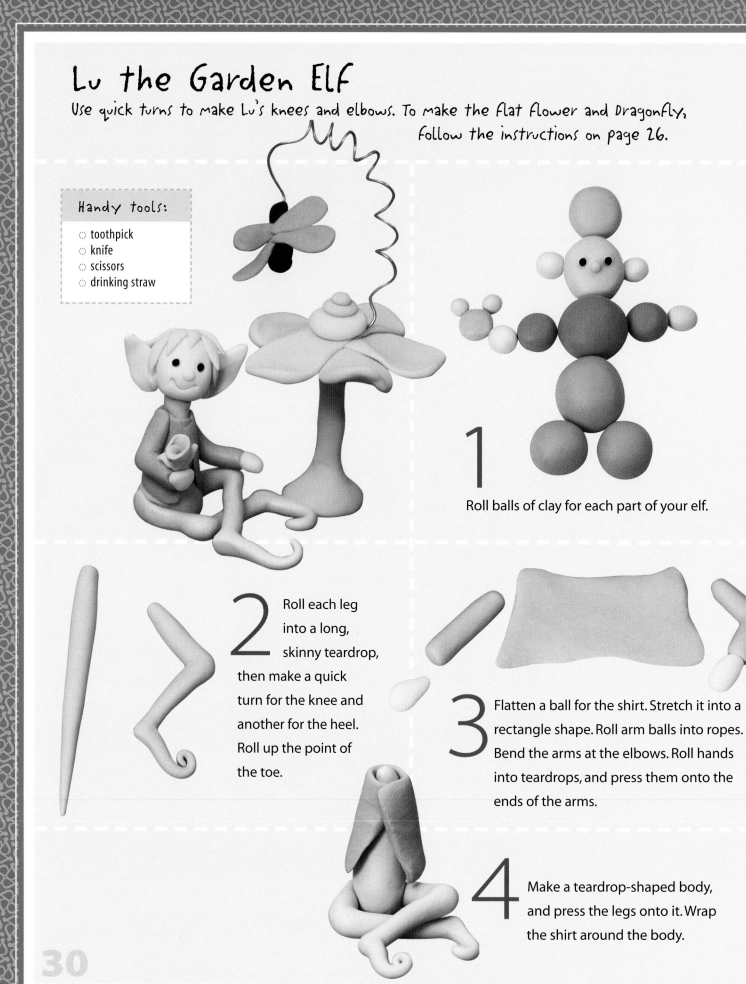

Handy tools:
- toothpick
- knife
- scissors
- drinking straw

1
Roll balls of clay for each part of your elf.

2
Roll each leg into a long, skinny teardrop, then make a quick turn for the knee and another for the heel. Roll up the point of the toe.

3
Flatten a ball for the shirt. Stretch it into a rectangle shape. Roll arm balls into ropes. Bend the arms at the elbows. Roll hands into teardrops, and press them onto the ends of the arms.

4
Make a teardrop-shaped body, and press the legs onto it. Wrap the shirt around the body.

5 Flatten the ball for the flower, then roll it tightly along one side. Make teardrop-shaped leaves, then flatten them. Wrap the leaves around the flower.

6 Attach the arms and press the flower into one hand. Break a piece of toothpick, and push it in for the neck.

7 Make a mouth with a piece of drinking straw (see page 41). Flatten teardrops for the ears, and press them onto the head with a tool. Use balls for the eyes and nose.

8 Make hair from flattened teardrops and press them in place. Follow the baking directions on page 5.

Be Creative!

How are these elves different from Lu? Making their hair longer and twisted makes them seem like new characters.

Making Hollow Shapes

You can use many different tools for hollowing. Some that work well are a paintbrush handle, a wooden dowel with the end rounded with sandpaper, a thick knitting needle or an unsharpened pencil rounded with sandpaper.

1
Make a shape, like a cone, then insert a tool halfway into it.

2
Hold the clay still with one hand. Push the tool down and roll it back and forth. Don't let the clay move.

3
When one part is thin, turn the shape to a new spot and roll the tool again.

4
Stretch the clay with your fingers to make it even thinner.

More Ways

When making a round hollow shape, hold the clay and use a tool to begin hollowing. Then press with your fingers to make the sides thin.

Mouths, ears and eyes are also hollowed shapes. Choose a tool that is slightly smaller than the size of the hole.

Baby Bear

Practice making hollow shapes as you make Baby Bear.

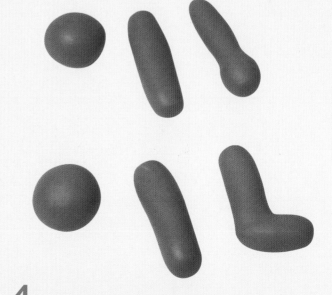

Handy tools:
- toothpick
- hollowing tool
  (see page 32)

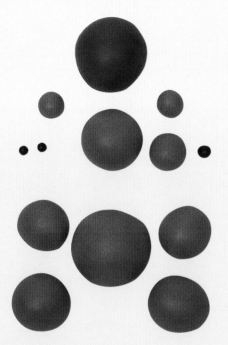

1 Begin by making the clay balls for each part of Baby Bear.

2 Roll the body ball into an egg shape. Insert half a toothpick.

3 Roll the ball for Baby Bear's snout into a cone shape. Press it onto the ball for the his head. Hollow out his mouth and eyes with a skinny paintbrush handle or a toothpick. Then press on the balls for the eyes and nose.

4 Roll skinny drumsticks for the arms. For each leg, make a rope with a quick turn to make a heel.

continued on the next page ➜ **33**

5   Press on the legs and head. Make a cone for the hat and hollow it. The two balls that are left are for ears.

6   Place the hat on the head. Press the ears onto the hat. Hollow the ears with a paintbrush handle. Follow the baking directions on page 5.

Teacup

A teacup is just a hollow ball with a handle. Make one for your Baby Bear.

1   Start with a ball and a skinny rope for the handle. Hollow the ball by pressing and rolling the tool, not the clay.

2   Press the handle onto the cup. If the handle is too small to hold with your fingers, try picking it up with a tool, such as a knitting needle. Follow the baking directions on page 5.

More Bears

All these bears have hollowed parts, too.

These hats are cones that were hollowed with different tools. The smaller the hat, the smaller the hollowing tool.

To make sleeves, hollow the end of a rope and insert balls for hands.

This bear has hollowed balls for his hat and pants and hollowed ropes for his pant legs. His feet are stuck into his pant legs.

Doing the
Drumstick Roll

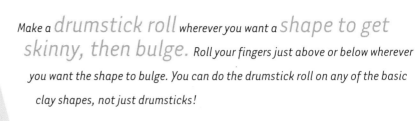

Make a drumstick roll *wherever you want a* shape to get skinny, then bulge. *Roll your fingers just above or below wherever you want the shape to bulge. You can do the drumstick roll on any of the basic clay shapes, not just drumsticks!*

slim the slug

Once you can make a drumstick roll, changing it to a slug is easy. To make a snail, just roll up the slug's body!

Handy tools:

- colored wire
- tools to make a mouth (see page 41)

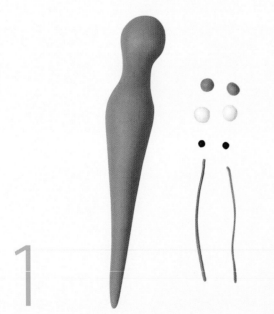

1 Make a long, skinny ghost shape using a single drumstick roll at the neck. Then make balls for the eyelids, eyeballs and pupils. Use wire for the antennae.

2 Bend the ghost shape at the neck and tail. Roll the eyelids into football shapes. Curl the antennae ends.

3 Add a nose and a mouth using a tool (see pages 41-42). Make the eyes and press onto the head. Flatten the eyelids.

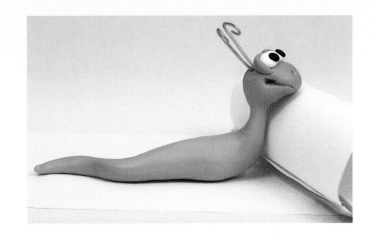

4 Wrap a flattened eyelid around the top of each eyeball. Add antennae. Prop the head with an index card while baking. Bake following the directions on page 5.

Lightening the Lizard
You can make a lizard with five drumstick rolls!

Handy tools:
- tools to make a mouth (see page 41)

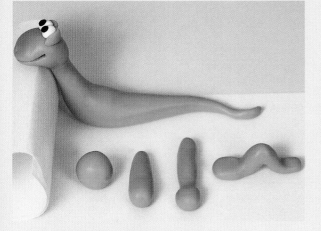

1 Begin with a slug, but do not attach antennae. Make small, skinny drumstick shapes for legs.

2 Press the legs onto the belly of the lizard.

3 Prop the head while baking. Bake following the directions on page 5.

37

Trundle the Turtle

By adding a shell, your lizard can become a turtle!

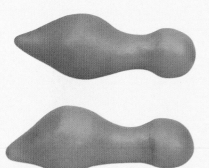

1 To make a turtle, shorten the tail on the lizard. Flatten a ball for the shell.

2 Bake following the directions on page 5.

Franklin the Frog

Meet Franklin! With some drumstick rolls and a few quick turns, he's easy to make.

Handy tools:

○ toothpick

1 Franklin begins as a lizard. Remove almost all of the tail, and flatten the body and the head a little bit.

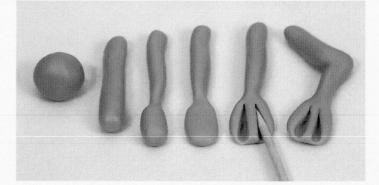

2 Make the front legs as shown. Use a toothpick to make the webbing marks.

3 Make the two back legs in the same way, but notice that the back legs are longer, with two quick turns instead of one. Add eyes, a nose and a mouth (see pages 41–43).

Be Creative!

Here are Franklin's friends. Changing the pose changes the personality of the character. Add that idea to your bag of clay tricks!

making
FACES

Head Shapes
When you're making up your own characters, you may want to start by choosing a shape for the character's head. These are the most common shapes and some ideas to get you started.

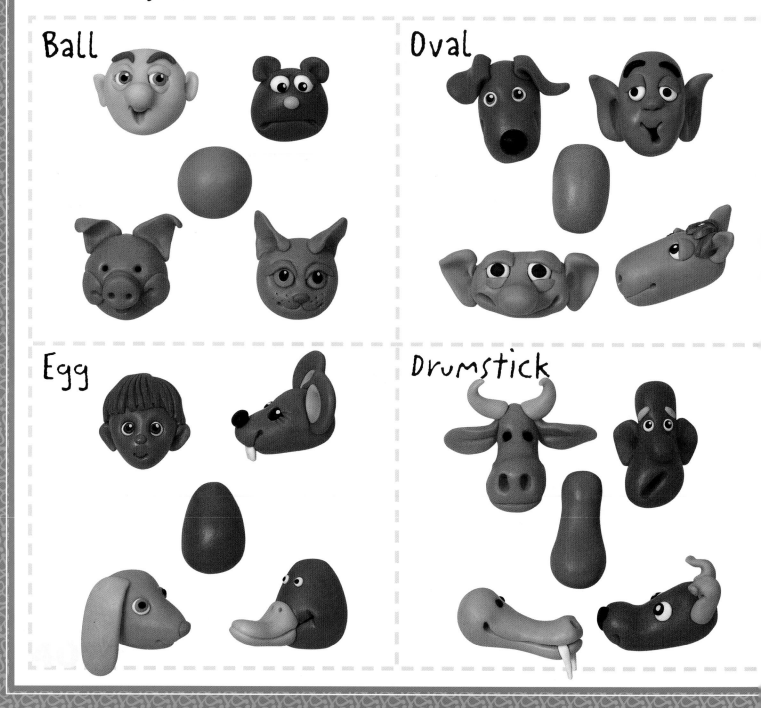

Ball

Oval

Egg

Drumstick

Mouths
After you make the head shape, you'll make the mouth.

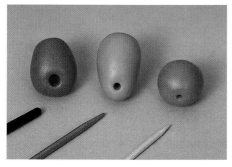

Mouths can be *poked holes.*

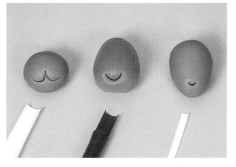

Or they can be *pressed-in lines.*

A cut and curved piece of *index card* or a *drinking straw* cut the long way makes a good mouth.

Another Way

1 To give mouths lots of expression, use a tool to make a deep hole.

2 Then gently press and pat it to close the corners.

3 Press in slightly at the spot where the mouth meets the cheek.

Be Creative!

Wide open mouths can be cut open, hollowed out slightly, then closed and patted into shape. Try twisting the mouth into different expressions.

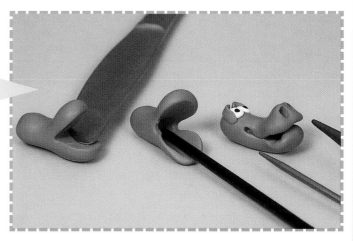

Noses

Here are lots of ideas for making noses.

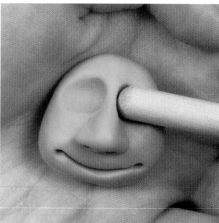

Noses can be just holes *poked into the face.*

Noses can be teardrop or rounded shapes *that are pressed into place.*

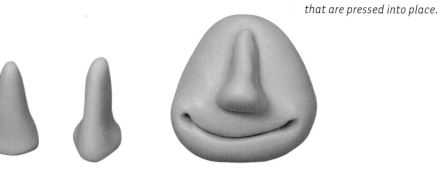

A nose may begin as a cone *that is* pinched *into a nose shape. You can leave it like this.*

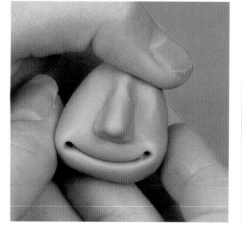

Or you can use your finger to blend *the* top *of it into the head. This will make it look* more realistic.

If you like, you can roll and press *a rounded tool against the nose to blend the sides of the nose. This creates a* bridge *to the nose and also makes a place for the* eyes.

Eyes

By changing the eyes or eyelids on a character, you can change what that character is feeling or thinking.

Here are two ways to make eyes. The eyes on the left start with a white ball of clay, then a black clay ball is pressed onto it. The eyes on the right start with a white ball, then a small colored ball is added, followed by a tiny black ball for the pupil.

The last thing to add is the sparkle in the eyes. Make some really tiny balls of white clay. Place one to the left or right side of each eye, but not in the middle. If the sparkle is too big, the character will look blind.

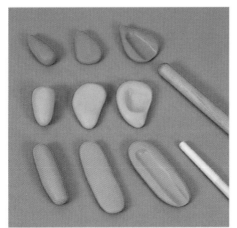

Eyelids can make the character look surprised, worried, angry or sleepy. The expression depends on how much of the eye is covered and the angle of the eyelid.

hint... **Another type of eye is just a round black ball of clay. It's a good idea to make dozens of these and bake them ahead of time. Because they're baked, they will stay round when you press them into place.**

Ears

What kind of ears will your creatures have? Here are a few to choose from.

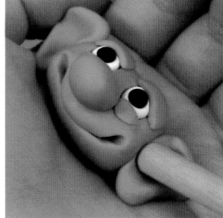

Make the shape that you want for the ear. Flatten it slightly, then shape it by pressing and rolling a tool in the center.

Put the ear in place, then press it with a rounded tool to make sure it stays put.

the magic of
STORYCLAY

So much you've learned!

You've learned how to hollow, to roll and to twist.
You've learned faces, made spaces, flattened and mixed.

You've made funny characters, but what to do now?
How about names for the pig and the cow?

How about homes for the small and the tall?
How about stories just right for them all?

Stories that don't have to end with a rhyme.
OK? Let's get started. It's Storyclay time!

Now read the **story** of Thistledown Will
and his friends and use what you've learned
to make these
characters and
many more!

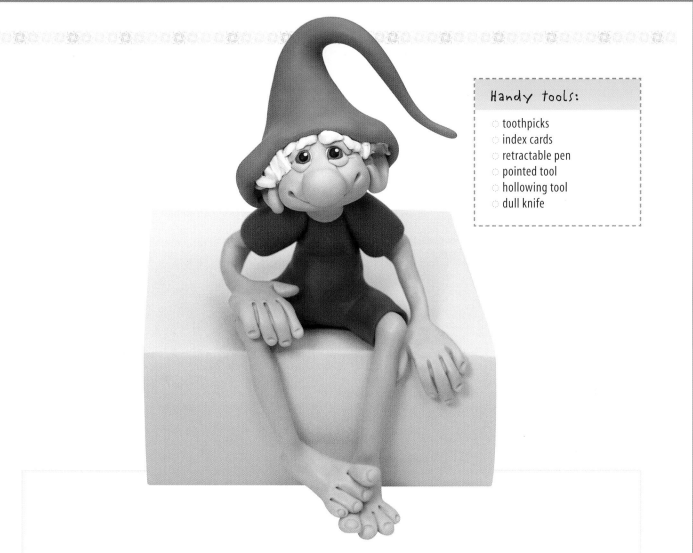

Handy tools:
- toothpicks
- index cards
- retractable pen
- pointed tool
- hollowing tool
- dull knife

❦ CHAPTER ONE ❦

How Dragon Got His Scales Back

Thistledown Will is a troll. He lives in a sturdy little house with a wooden front door and two shuttered windows, one on each side of the door. His house is tucked in among the gnarled and twisted roots of an old willow tree that grows on the banks of a small winding creek. Thistledown Will loves mysteries—and, though he doesn't know it, one is about to begin.

continued on the next page ➡

Thistledown Will

1 Begin by rolling a ball into an egg to make the body and neck.

2 Make ropes for the legs and make a quick turn for the foot. Flatten the foot and make a quick turn for the knee. Roll small pieces of clay into egg shapes for the toes.

3 Attach the legs to the egg-shaped body. Use a tool like a pen to make toenails.

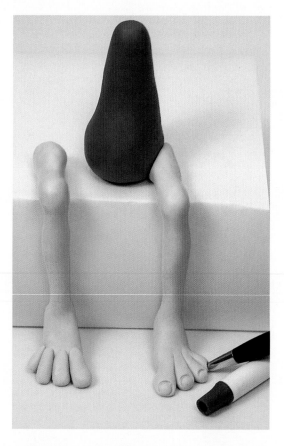

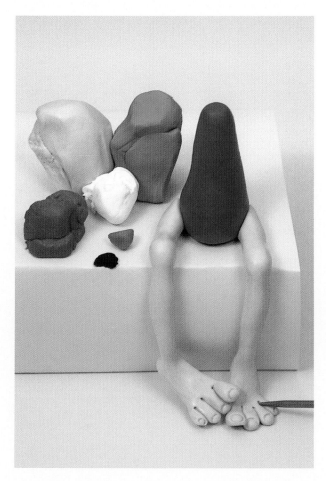

4 Pick out some colors for the other parts of Thistledown Will. Use a pointed tool, like a knitting needle or toothpick, to make the lines between his toes.

5 Roll the hat into a ball, then an egg, then a teardrop, then a cone. Flatten the hair and the pant legs. Use a knife to cut lines for the hair and a tool to hollow out the egg-shaped sleeves.

continued on the next page ➡

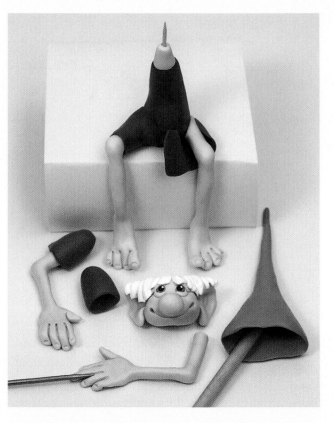

6 Roll clay into balls and then eggs for the head, nose and ears. Choose colors for the eyes and roll each part into a ball. Begin the arms as ropes, then make a drumstick roll to create the wrist and hand. Flatten the hands. For fingers, make short ropes, then press them in place and blend the seam with your thumb.

7 Wrap the flattened pant legs around each leg. Make a quick turn for each elbow, then press the arms into the sleeves. Use a piece of index card to make the mouth. Flatten the ears slightly and press the nose, eyes, eyelids, ears and hair into place, in that order. Hollow out the hat, then put the parts together. Bake as directed on page 5.

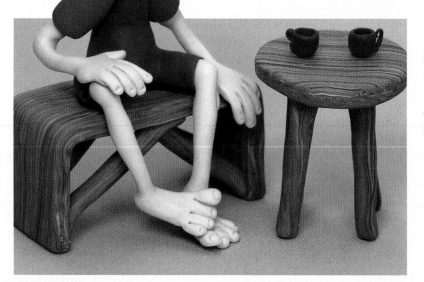

*To make a **table and bench** for Thistledown Will, follow the directions on page 78. Instructions for the teacups are on page 34.*

Handy tools:

- hollowing tool
- paintbrush handle or knitting needle
- toothpick
- dull knife

☙ CHAPTER TWO ❧

A Troublesome Find

Just down the river from Thistledown Will lives Rainbow Goblin. He and his six goblin friends live in a cave under the waterfall. Every day they stand at their windows with little nets, straining the water as it rushes by. One never knows what tiny treasures might be floating in the stream. Once, the Rainbow Goblin found a diamond ring, and, on another day, a shiny gold charm that was shaped like a key. He always wondered if it was the key to anything special.

One day the Rainbow Goblin sent a note to the Troll, Thistledown Will. The note said:

The creek is almost dry. I will come to your place on Tuesday at three in the afternoon to show you a troublesome thing. Pig and Hen are coming with me.
Sincerely, Rainbow Goblin

continued on the next page ➡

Rainbow Goblin

how to make

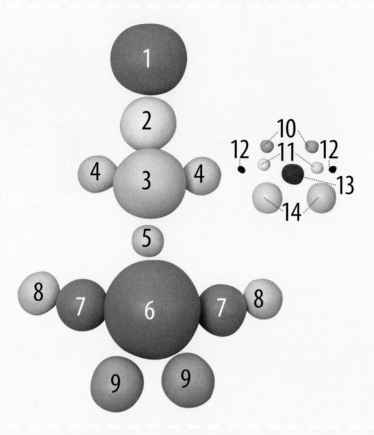

1. Make these balls of clay for the Rainbow Goblin:

1	hat
2	hair
3	head
4	ears
5	neck
6	body (robe)
7	sleeves
8	hands
9	legs and feet
10	eyelids
11	eyeballs
12	pupils
13	nose
14	cheeks

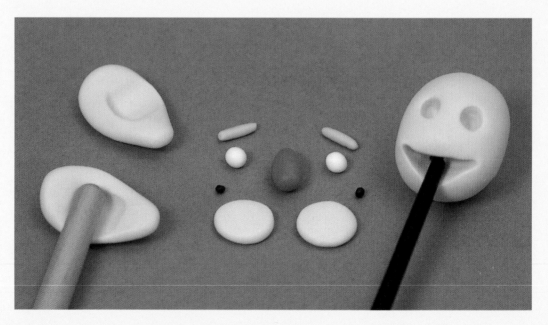

2. Roll the ear balls into egg shapes, then flatten them slightly. Hollow with a rounded tool. Flatten the cheek balls. Roll the eyebrow balls into football shapes. Press in eye sockets with the end of a paintbrush. Use a paintbrush handle or knitting needle to make the mouth.

3

Press on the eyes, nose and cheeks. Draw in the mouth with a sharp tool. Press a rounded tool into the corner of the mouth to create dimples.

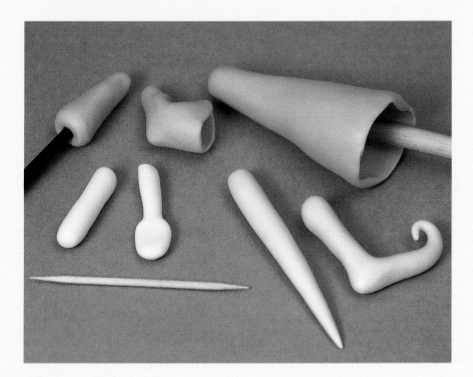

4

Roll sleeve and robe balls into long, skinny eggs, then hollow them with a paintbrush handle. With the sleeve still on handle, make a quick turn in the sleeve for the elbow. Roll the hand balls into ropes, then do a drumstick roll to create wrists. Flatten the hands. Begin the shoes with a ball, then roll each into an egg and a long, skinny teardrop. Do a quick turn for the heel, then roll up the toes. The toothpick is for his backbone.

continued on the next page ➡

51

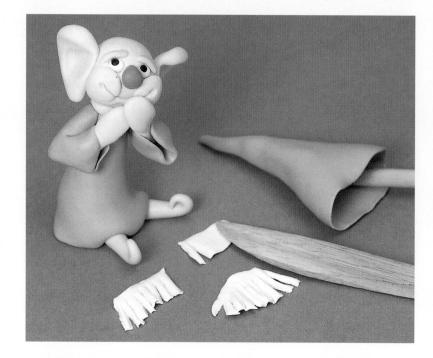

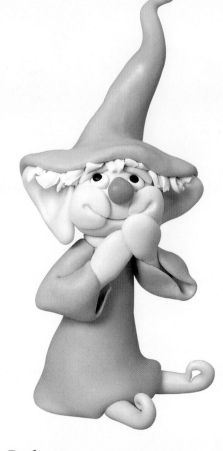

5 Press the feet into the hollowed robe and the hands into the hollowed sleeves. Stand up Goblin, then press on sleeves. Press in toothpick backbone. Press on head and ears. Add pupils and eyebrows. Roll the hat ball into an egg, then a teardrop, then a long cone. Hollow out the hat. Flatten the hair and cut in lines with a clay-sculpting tool or a dull knife. Press on the hair and hat.

Bake *Rainbow Goblin following the instructions on page 5.*

Be Creative!

Here are some more goblins you can make. Or create some of your own!

Handy tools:

◌ aluminum foil
◌ toothpicks
◌ dull knife
◌ index card
◌ knitting needle
◌ paintbrush handle

❖ CHAPTER THREE ❖

Dragon Scales

At three o'clock sharp on Tuesday afternoon, Thistledown Will saw the Rainbow Goblin, Pig and Hen come running along the edge of the creek. Without even stopping to drink the tea or sample the cookies that Thistledown Will had laid out for them, they began chattering about dragon scales and the world changing and nothing ever being the same again.

Rainbow Goblin laid his backpack on the steps and opened it to reveal a beautiful, shiny dragon scale. Thistledown Will looked startled. "How did you get this, and what does it mean?"

"I caught it in my net last Friday," said Rainbow Goblin, "and on Saturday I found another!"

"We are worried that Dragon is dying," cried Pig and Hen. "There's always been a dragon near our creek. Every great adventure has a dragon in it somewhere! Dragons keep things from getting boring. No dragons, no great stories, no wondrous heroes. We wouldn't like a world without dragons."

By now, Thistledown Will was worried. "Rainbow Goblin, you go back to the falls and keep watch for more dragon scales. Pig and Hen, you run to the forest and search for Forest Elf. He will know what to do."

continued on the next page ➡

how to make Pig

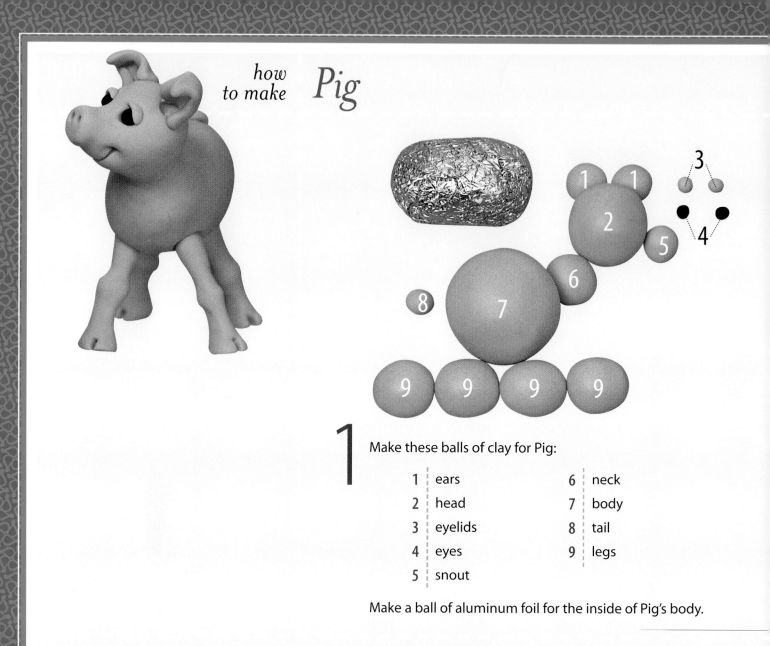

1

Make these balls of clay for Pig:

1	ears	6	neck
2	head	7	body
3	eyelids	8	tail
4	eyes	9	legs
5	snout		

Make a ball of aluminum foil for the inside of Pig's body.

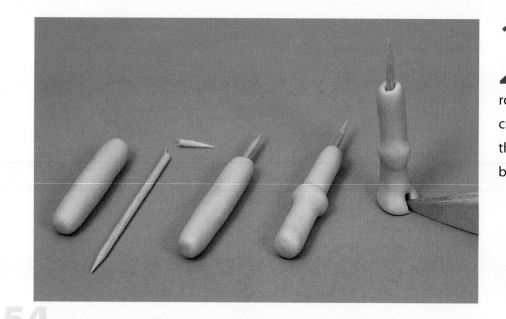

2

Roll the legs into ropes. Insert a toothpick into each. Do a drumstick roll on each side of the knee to create a bulge. Press the hoof to the work surface to flatten the bottom. Cut in a split-hoof line.

3

Bake the legs in the aluminum foil body. Let them cool completely.

4

Remove the cooled legs. Cover the foil body with clay. Attach the snout to the head. Notice that the neck and eye pieces are not yet attached.

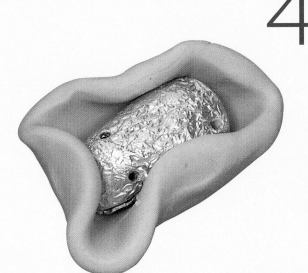

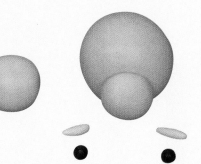

continued on the next page ➡

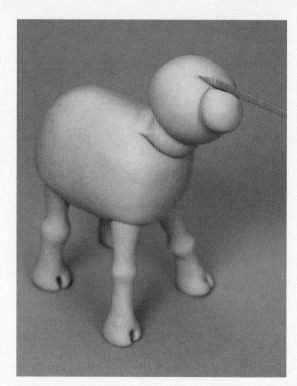

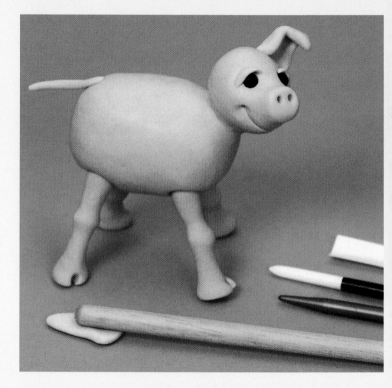

5 Add the legs. Attach the head and neck to the body. You can put the pieces together and not smooth the seam lines. Or you can use your thumb or a rounded tool to blend the places where the parts are joined.

6 Roll each ear into a cone shape, then flatten. Hollow it with a rounded tool, then press into place. Use a knitting needle to make the nostrils and a paintbrush handle to make the eye sockets. Use the index card to make the mouth. Make a skinny rope for the tail.

Bake Pig *following*

the instructions on page 5.

how to make # Hen

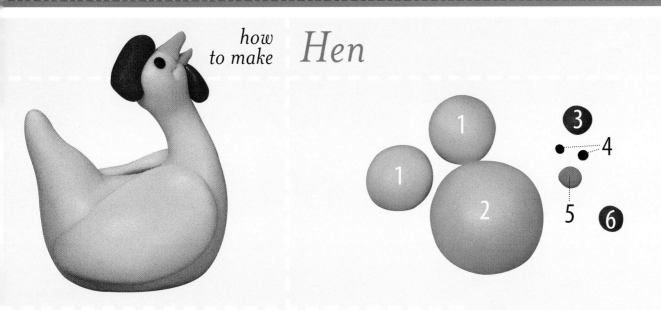

1 Make these balls of clay for Hen:

1	wings
2	body and head
3	comb
4	eyes
5	beak
6	wattle

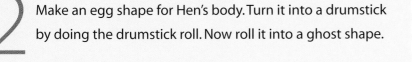

2 Make an egg shape for Hen's body. Turn it into a drumstick by doing the drumstick roll. Now roll it into a ghost shape.

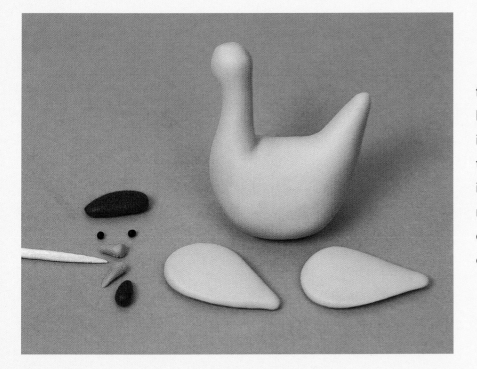

3 Bend the ghost shape to form a head and tail. Roll two eggs for wings, then flatten them. Form the parts for the head. Because the beak is so small, it is easier to put it on the end of the toothpick, then press the toothpick into the face. Roll the toothpick to release the beak. Add the comb and eyes. Bake following the instructions on page 5.

57

CHAPTER FOUR

Forest Elf Helps Out

Pig and Hen found Forest Elf sitting in a giant oak tree reading a book.

"Elf, Elf," they shouted. "Have you heard that Rainbow Goblin has found dragon scales floating down the stream? We are worried that the world is changing!"

Forest Elf jumped up. "I will go in search of Dragon's cousins, the Sea Serpents. They'll know what is happening. You go back and tell the others to come to the waterfall when they hear thirteen strokes of the bell."

And he took off running through the trees.

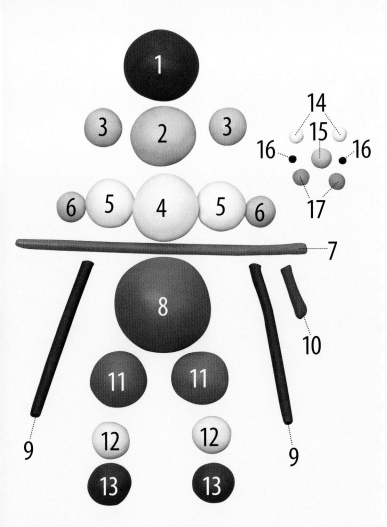

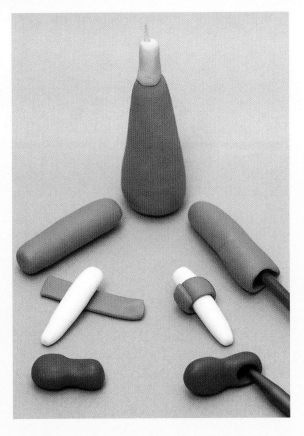

Make these balls of clay for the Forest Elf:

1	hair	10	buttons
2	head	11	pant legs
3	ears	12	socks
4	shirt	13	shoes
5	sleeves	14	eyes
6	hands	15	nose
7	belt	16	pupils
8	body	17	cheeks
9	suspenders		

2 Roll the body into a tall egg shape. Press in a toothpick for the neck. Add the neck. Make ropes for the legs and socks. Hollow the legs. For cuff, wrap an extra strip of pants-colored clay around top of socks. Form small drumstick shapes for the shoes. Use a tool to hollow out the hole in the shoe.

continued on the next page ➡

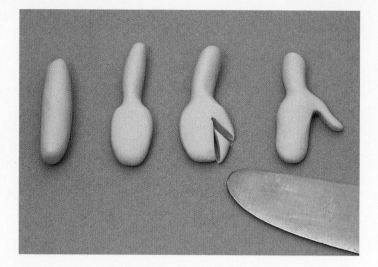

3 Make a rope for the hands, then a skinny drumstick. Flatten the hands. Cut out a piece of each hand to make a thumb. Use your fingers to smooth the thumb.

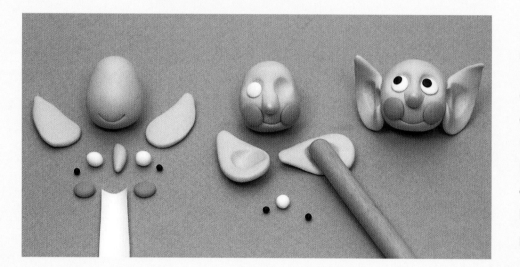

4 Make shapes for the head. Flatten egg shapes for the ears. Make the mouth with a curved index card. Add the nose. Use a rounded tool to hollow space for eyes on each side of the nose. Also hollow the ears. Press all parts into place.

5 Press socks into legs, then press legs onto body. Add the head on top of the tooth-pick. Flatten the shirt piece into a rectangle. Roll the sleeves into ropes, then hollow each.

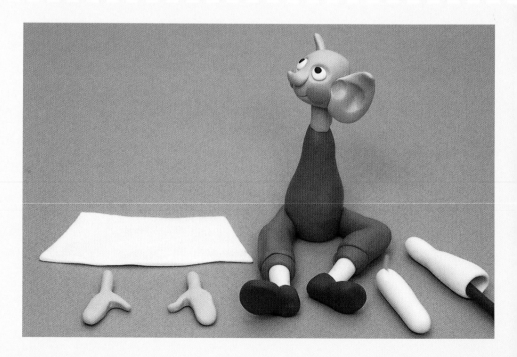

6 Wrap the shirt around the body, overlapping in front. Stretch it if it is too small. Press the hands into the sleeves, then onto the body. Roll and flatten the suspenders and belt. Roll tiny balls for buttons.

7 A garlic press is a great way to make hair. Remember, once it's used for clay, you shouldn't use it again for food. If you don't have a garlic press, use your imagination to make Elf's hair another way. Use a toothpick to remove hair from the garlic press, then press a toothpick, with the hair still on it, onto the head. Roll the toothpick to release the hair.

Bake *Forest Elf following the instructions on page 5.*

61

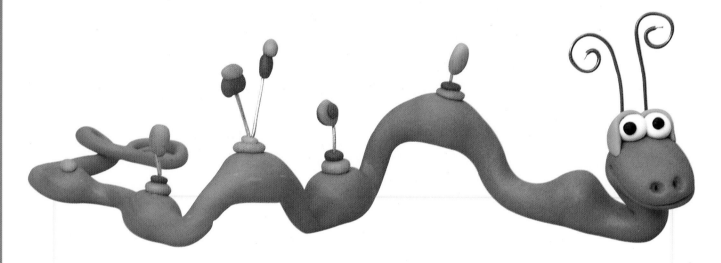

◈ CHAPTER FIVE ◈

The Dragon's Cousins

Forest Elf found the Sea Serpents sunning themselves on rocks near where the deepest pools in the creek were still full of water. "Do you know what is happening to Dragon?" he asked.

The biggest serpent looked lazily at Elf and said, "Last we heard he was hiding. We heard him muttering something about not being able to fly anymore. Humpfffffffff! We don't know what is so bad about that! Why don't you ask Dog and Cat to use their tracking and prowling skills to find him? We can't be bothered."

And they went back to lying lazily in the sun.

Sea Serpents

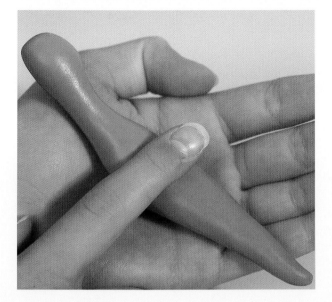

1 Start with a ball of clay. Roll body into an egg shape, then into a drumstick. Roll the fat end into a long, skinny ghost shape.

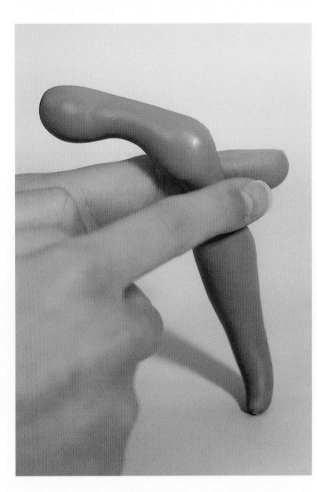

2 Do a drumstick roll each place where you want a bulge to be, then do another one on the other side of the bulge.

continued on the next page ➡

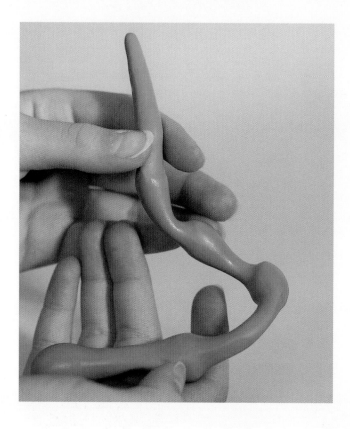

3 Continue making bulges along the whole length of Sea Serpent.

4 Draw in a mouth and add balls for the eyes. Add flattened footballs for eyebrows.

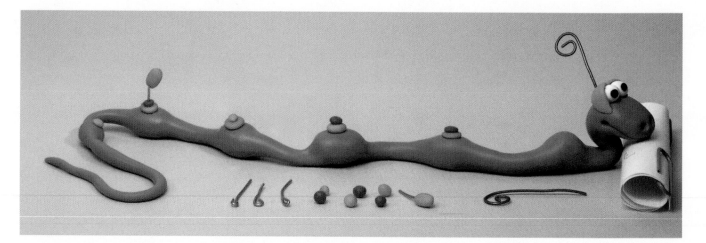

5 Roll tiny balls of different colored clay. Press some balls onto the body, layering colors if you like. Cut wires. Bend one end of each wire to make a loop. These loops will keep the clay balls from slipping off. Press balls of clay over loops, then press wires into body. The wire used in this project is 24-gauge plastic-coated wire. Other wire you can use includes straightened paper clips or colored wire from a craft store.

6 Before baking, prop Sea Serpent on rolled index cards like this.

Bake Sea Serpent following the instructions on page 5.

Be **Creative!**

Here are some more sea serpents for you to make.

CHAPTER SIX

Dog and Cat Find Dragon

 og and Cat, being very secretive, never told anyone how they found Dragon, but it is true that they did.

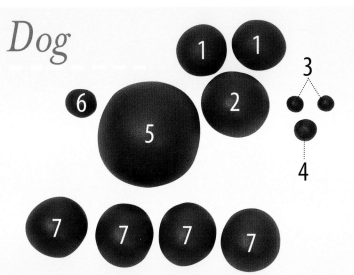

how to make *Dog*

Make these balls of clay for Dog:

1 | ears
2 | head
3 | eyes
4 | nose
5 | body
6 | tail
7 | legs

2 Make a long, skinny egg for Dog's body. Turn up the end slightly for the neck. Add half of a toothpick. Start each leg as a thick rope, then roll into a drumstick. Make a quick turn for the heel. Add toothpicks. Flatten each foot. Press in lines with a knife. Roll a rope for the tail.

3 Roll skinny egg shapes for the head and ears. Poke holes for eyes. Flatten the ears. Hollow the center of the ears with a rounded tool. Make the eyes, nose and eyelids.

4 Press the legs into the body, then the tail. Use a sharp tool to make the mouth. Add eyes and ears. Press the head onto the body and add the nose. Prop Dog's head on a ball of foil while baking. Place a piece of paper towel between the head and the foil. Bake. Cool. To make Dog's nose and eyes shiny, brush on gloss lacquer that is made especially for polymer clay.

continued on the next page ➔ **67**

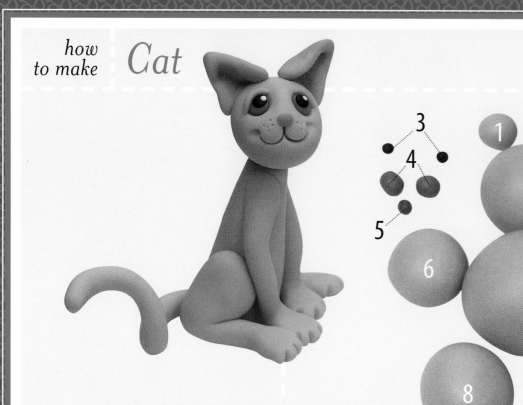

1 Make these balls of clay for Cat:

1	ears	6	front legs
2	head	7	body
3	pupils	8	back legs (make one more
4	eyeballs		ball this size for the tail)
5	nose		

2

Make a rope for each of Cat's legs. Do a drumstick roll at one end to make a paw, then flatten slightly and add toe marks. Keep front legs straight. Do a quick turn in the middle of each back leg. Make a rope for the tail. Make a skinny egg for the body.

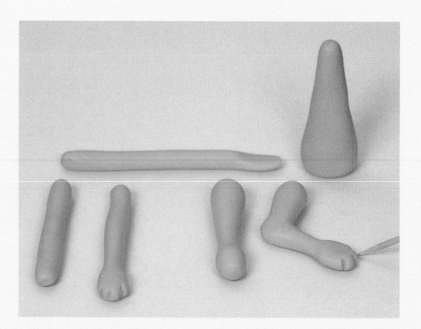

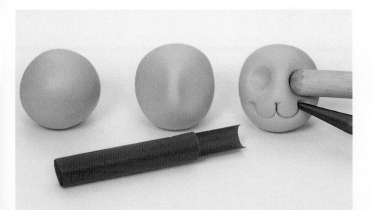

3 Make two thumb prints in the middle of the head to create a nose shape. Press in eye sockets with a rounded tool. Use a cut drinking straw to make two curves for the mouth. Press mouth corners with a knitting needle to make dimples.

4 Press the legs and tail onto the body. Add a toothpick for the neck, then press on the head. Add ears, eyes and eyelids. Use a toothpick to make whisker holes. Prop the tail while baking. Bake following the instructions on page 5.

Be Creative!

To make a cat that is lying down, make an egg-shaped body and use shorter legs.

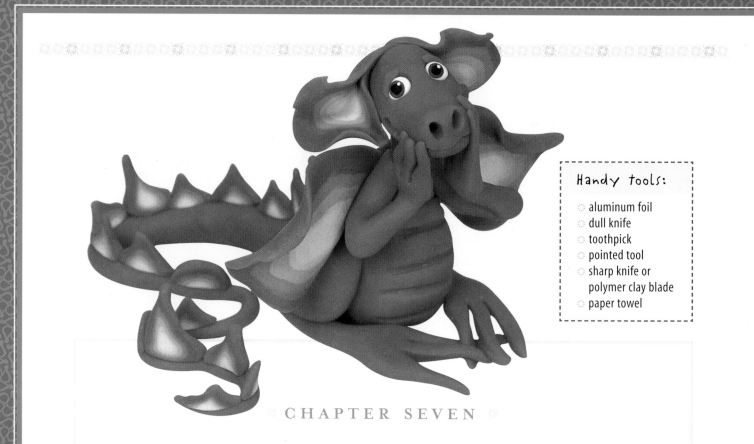

CHAPTER SEVEN

How Dragon Lost His Scales

Thistledown Will was eating his morning toast when he heard the bells begin to ring. He cocked his head to count. "One, two, three … eleven, twelve, thirteen." Yes, it had rung thirteen times. He dropped his toast and was already running by the time he reached the front door.

At the waterfall, he found Cat, Dog, the Sea Serpents, Forest Elf, Pig, Hen and Rainbow Goblin already there. Seated beside Elf was his friend, Flower Fairy. Elf explained what Dog and Cat had discovered about Dragon. "Dragon was flying low over the river trying to scare a pair of field mice when he flew too low under the electric wires and knocked two scales off his tail.

"Splash! The scales fell into the water and away they went, over the falls and out of sight. Dragon landed safely by the side of the creek, but when he tried to lift his wings and fly, nothing happened. With those two scales missing, he was grounded!

"He hid under a bush. Then, during the night, he crawled back to his cave. Flying is like food and energy to a dragon. If he doesn't fly soon, he will begin to dry up and die."

how to make Dragon

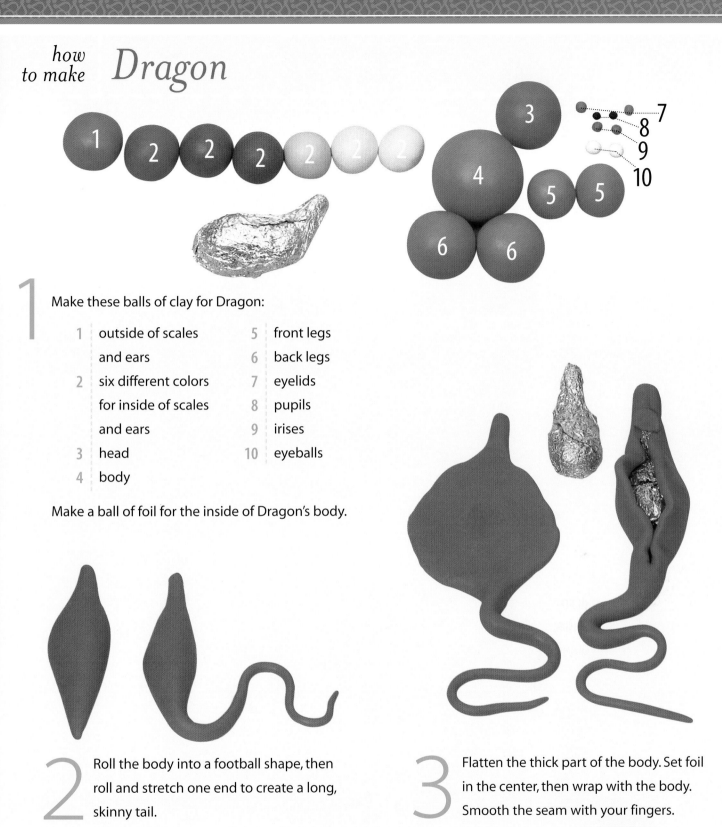

1

Make these balls of clay for Dragon:

1	outside of scales and ears	5	front legs
2	six different colors for inside of scales and ears	6	back legs
		7	eyelids
		8	pupils
3	head	9	irises
4	body	10	eyeballs

Make a ball of foil for the inside of Dragon's body.

2

Roll the body into a football shape, then roll and stretch one end to create a long, skinny tail.

3

Flatten the thick part of the body. Set foil in the center, then wrap with the body. Smooth the seam with your fingers.

continued on the next page →

71

4 Make Dragon's front and back feet the same, but make the back feet much larger. Roll each into a long, skinny egg, then a drumstick. Do a quick turn in the center of each for knees and elbows. Press foot to flatten. Cut in toes. Roll each toe to make it skinny.

5 Set the body on work surface. Turn the neck so that it points up. Press in a toothpick. Press on legs. Make lines on his chest. Roll a short drumstick for the head. Draw in mouth and press in holes for the eyes and nostrils.

6 Press on the head. For eyes, add white balls, then smaller balls of colored clay, black clay and a speck of white. Add football-shaped eyelids. Position him on an index card, but don't bake yet.

7 To make the scales, start with a rope of clay. Flatten other colors of clay to rectangles. Roll the flat pieces of clay around the rope.

8 Roll this big tube of clay slightly to blend the layers. While the tube is still thick, ask an adult to use a sharp knife or polymer clay blade to cut off a thick section for wings. Roll and stretch the remaining tube to make it skinnier. Slice off a section for ears. Roll and stretch the rest of the tube so that it is the size needed for scales, and slice. Shape wings, ears and scales, flattening them as needed to make them thin. Cut the scales in half, then pinch to a point.

9 Press the scales, wings and ears in place. Notice that the tops of the ears are folded. Curl edges slightly. If necessary, support wings while baking against a ball of foil that is covered with paper toweling. Bake.

The expression on this dragon's face fits this story. The dragon you make can be friendly or scary to fit your own story.

73

◈ CHAPTER EIGHT ◈

Flower Fairy to the Rescue

Pig and Hen shook their heads. "This will never do, never do," they muttered.

Cat asked, "Since Rainbow Goblin was lucky enough to find the two Dragon scales, can't someone just sew them back on to Dragon's tail?"

"Ah," said the Forest Elf, "but who will do it?" They all looked at each other. Who would volunteer? It was one thing to admire and respect a dragon, but quite another to perch on its back and sew through its skin!

There was silence. Then Flower Fairy began to speak. "I have often been bored with the stories told about fairies. I am more than sweet. I am more than beauty. I have longed to test my courage against a dragon. I will do it." With that, she calmly smiled and flew off with the two dragon scales.

That night, Thistledown Will settled contentedly onto his front step. He had just seen Dragon fly overhead. And he had just received a new story from Pig. It began, "Once upon a time, there was a dragon...and a fairy...." *THE END*

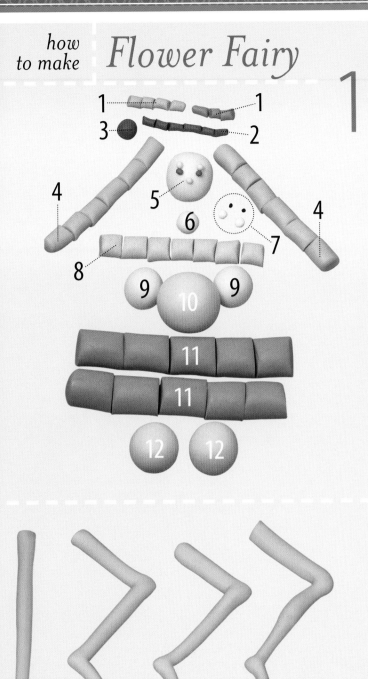

how
to make **Flower Fairy**

1. Make these balls and ropes of clay for Flower Fairy:

1	flowers	7	eyes
2	leaves	8	petals for blouse
3	wreath	9	arms
4	hair	10	body
5	head	11	petals for skirt
6	neck	12	legs

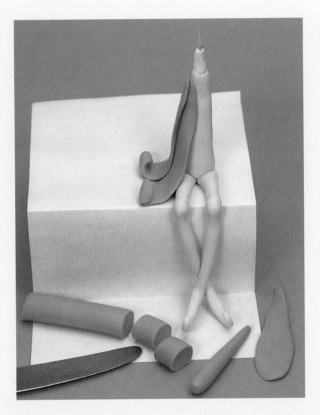

3. Set Fairy on a square cardboard box that is covered with an index card. Roll a long, skinny egg shape for her body. Press in a toothpick backbone. Add a neck. Shape the petals for her dress like long teardrops, then flatten. Press on each, then curl the ends.

2. Each leg begins as a long, skinny cone shape. Make one quick turn for the knee and a second for the heel. Roll up the toe and curve the foot.

continued on the next page →

75

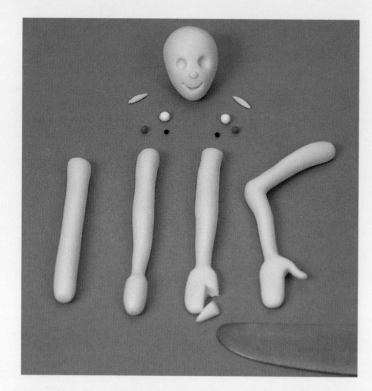

4 Make an egg-shaped head, white, blue and black balls for eyes, footballs for eyelids and ropes for arms. Do a drumstick roll to make wrists. Flatten hands slightly, then cut out a section to shape the thumb. Make a quick turn for the elbow.

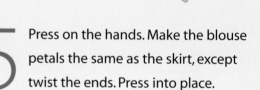

5 Press on the hands. Make the blouse petals the same as the skirt, except twist the ends. Press into place.

6 Add the head. Make hair the same as skirt and shirt petals, except slightly skinnier. Make some hairs long and some shorter.

7 For wreath, wrap a thin green rope around the head. Flatten teardrops for leaves. Press in place with a toothpick. For flowers, roll a short rope. Flatten it, then roll it up loosely like a jelly roll. Press flowers in place with a toothpick. Curl over edges with your finger. Bake following the instructions on page 5.

Turn to page 78 for instructions on how to make **this bench**.

Table and Bench

To give your characters a place to sit during their adventures, you can make a table and bench!

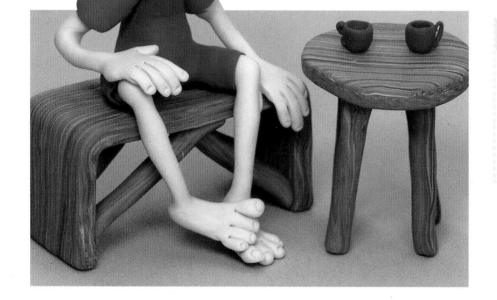

1 Cut open the cereal box to make a flat piece of cardboard. Draw a rectangle that is big enough to make a bench for your characters. Then add extra on each end for legs. Draw a circle pattern for a tabletop. Cut out both shapes. Fold the bench legs down.

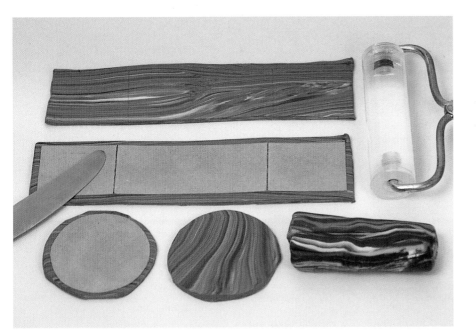

2 Mix up some brown, white and yellow clay until it looks like wood, then flatten it to the thickness of a wooden ruler. Cover the flattened bench and the table top on all sides with the clay mixture, leaving the cardboard inside. Use a toothpick to draw in rough wood lines.

3 Fold the bench legs again so that the clay-covered bench will stand, then turn it upside down. To support the bench so that it won't fall down, cover four tooth-picks with clay, then wedge them into each corner. Use four clay-covered toothpicks for table legs.

4 To support them while they bake in the oven, wad up aluminum foil and place it under the bench and table. Bake following the instructions on page 5. Directions for making teacups are on page 34.

Get creative
with these other fun books for kids!

You can make incredible crafts using materials found just outside your window! Learn how to create pressed flower bookmarks, clay tiles, leaf prints, pebble mosaics, nature mobiles and souvenir pillows. You can use collected leaves, rocks, feathers and other natural treasures.

ISBN-13: 978-1-58180-292-4, paperback, 64 pages, #32169
ISBN-10: 1-58180-292-7, paperback, 64 pages, #32169

Create an idyllic, polymer-clay world filled with beautiful fairies, playful sprites, clever gnomes and elves, wise wizards and misunderstood trolls. Whether you are new to polymer clay, or looking to improve your skills, this book of 15 polymer clay projects offers everything you need to know to unlock the characters in your imagination and bring the magic of the fairy to life.

ISBN-13: 978-1-58180-820-9, paperback, 128 pages, #33502
ISBN-10: 1-58180-820-8, paperback, 128 pages, #33502

Hey kids! You can create amazing creatures, incredible toys and wild gifts for your friends and family. All it takes is some paint, a few rocks and your imagination! Easy-to-follow pictures and instructions show you how to turn stones into something cool—racecars, bugs, lizards, teddy bears and more.

ISBN-13: 978-1-58180-255-9, paperback, 64 pages, #32085
ISBN-10: 1-58180-255-2, paperback, 64 pages, #32085

Oh, the things you can create with paper! Learn how to make paper stars, party streamers, lanterns, hanging baskets, paper beads, handmade books, and more. These crafts are perfect for parties, rainy days and gift giving, plus they're easy to do and fun to make.

ISBN-13: 978-1-58180-290-0, paperback, 64 pages, #32167
ISBN-10: 1-58180-290-0, paperback, 64 pages, #32167

These and other fun North Light books are available from your local art & craft retailer, bookstore or online supplier.